Pebble® Plus

KU-147-749

LET'S LOOK AT COUNTRIES

LET'S LOOK AT
NIGERIA

BY MARY MEINKING

raintree
a Capstone company — publishers for children

Raintree is an imprint of Capstone Global Library Limited, a company incorporated in England and Wales having its registered office at 264 Banbury Road, Oxford, OX2 7DY – Registered company number: 6695582

www.raintree.co.uk
myorders@raintree.co.uk

Edited by Jessica Server
Designed by Juliette Peters
Picture research by Jo Miller
Production by Laura Manthe
Originated by Capstone Global Library Ltd
Printed and bound in India

ISBN 978 1 4747 8451 1 (hardback)
ISBN 978 1 4747 8468 9 (paperback)

British Library Cataloguing in Publication Data
A full catalogue record for this book is available from the British Library.

Photo Credits
Dreamstime: Joshua Wanyama, 5; iStockphoto: Lingbeek, Cover Bottom, Cover Back, peeterv, 17; Newscom: Africa Media Online/Andrew Esiebo, 21, Eye Ubiquitous, 15, 16, Minden Pictures/Cyril Ruoso, 9; Science Source: Marcello Bertinetti, 7; Shutterstock: Ajibola Fasoia, 11, Bill Kret, Cover Top, 1, 3, Brendan van Son, Cover Middle, Fanfo, 13, Globe Turner, 22 (Inset), nale, 4 (map), Tayvay, 19, 22

CONTENTS

Where is Nigeria?

Nigeria is on the west coast of Africa. It is nearly four times as big as the United Kingdom. Nigeria's capital city is Abuja.

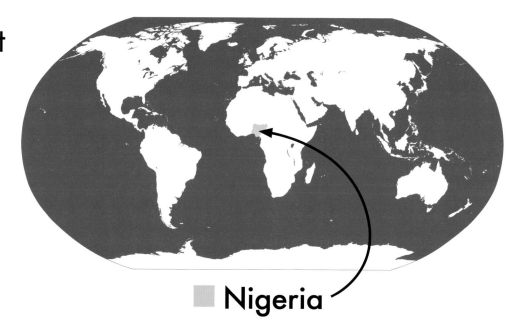

Nigeria

Abuja

From savannas to rivers

Northern Nigeria has large savannas. The south and east have mountains and rainforests. The Niger River runs through the country. It gave Nigeria its name.

In the wild

Many of Nigeria's animals live in protected parks. Elephants and antelope live on the savanna. Drill monkeys live in Nigerian forests. Crocodiles hunt in the rivers.

drill monkeys

People

People have lived in Nigeria for more than 10,000 years. More than 250 ethnic groups now live there. The largest groups are the Hausa, Yoruba and Igbo.

At the table

Nigerians eat soups with yams
or plantains. People also eat rice,
beans, fruit, fish and vegetables.
In the north people eat a grain
called millet. In the south they
eat Banga soup.

Banga soup

Festivals

The Argungu Fishing Festival is held in the north. Fishermen use nets to catch the biggest fish. They also have canoeing, swimming and other contests.

At work

Some Nigerians are farmers, fishermen or herdsmen. In cities many people work for big companies. Other people sell goods at markets.

Transport

People in Nigerian cities travel by car, taxi or van. Buses and trains run between cities. Many people use motorcycle taxis too.

motorcycle taxi

Famous place

Many tourists visit Nigeria's Osun Sacred Grove. Some people believe a goddess lives there. The forest has places for prayer and sculptures. Many years ago all villages had sacred groves.

QUICK NIGERIA FACTS

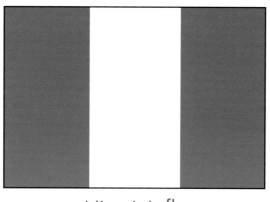
Nigeria's flag

Name: Federal Republic of Nigeria
Capital: Abuja
Other major cities: Lagos, Kano, and Ibadan
Population: 203,452,505 (July 2018 estimate)
Size: 923,768 sq km (356,669 square miles)
Language: English; hundreds of other languages spoken
Money: Nigerian naira

GLOSSARY

capital the city in a country where the government is based

ethnic having to do with a group of people sharing the same language, traditions and religion

grove a small wood, orchard or group of trees

herdsman a person who watches over cows, sheep or goats

plantain a tropical fruit that looks like a banana but cannot be eaten raw

protected to be kept safe from harm

sacred holy or having to do with religion

savanna a flat, grassy area of land with few or no trees

yam the root from a vine that grows in the tropics

FIND OUT MORE

Books

Living in Nigeria (Living in Africa), Annabelle Lynch (Franklin Watts, 2019)

Nigeria (Discover Countries), Alison Brownlie Bojang (Wayland, 2014)

Africa (Introducing Continents), Chris Oxlade and Anita Ganeri (Raintree, 2018)

Websites

Find out more facts and details about Nigeria at these great websites.

kids.britannica.com/kids/article/Nigeria/345758

www.activityvillage.co.uk/nigeria

www.sciencekids.co.nz/sciencefacts/countries/nigeria.html

COMPREHENSION QUESTIONS

1. If you lived in Nigeria, what job would you like to have? Why?

2. Name some animals that live in Nigeria. Which ones would you like to see most?

3. Do you think a motorcycle taxi would be better than a car taxi? Explain your answer.

INDEX